JESUS
REVEALED
IN THE
END TIMES

STUDY GUIDE

JESUS REVEALED IN THE END TIMES

STUDY GUIDE

*Hope for Today from the One
Who Holds Our Future*

Dr. Robert Jeffress

BakerBooks
a division of Baker Publishing Group
Grand Rapids, Michigan

Published by Baker Books
a division of Baker Publishing Group
Grand Rapids, Michigan
BakerBooks.com

Printed in the United States of America

Library of Congress Cataloging-in-Publication Data
Names: Jeffress, Robert, 1955– author.
Title: Jesus revealed in the end times study guide : hope for today from the one who holds our future / Dr. Robert Jeffress.
Description: Grand Rapids, Michigan : Baker Books, a division of Baker Publishing Group, [2025]
Identifiers: LCCN 2024035364 | ISBN 9781540903396 (paper) | ISBN 9781493449163 (ebook)
Subjects: LCSH: Jesus Christ—Person and offices—Study and teaching. | Jesus Christ—Prophecies—Study and teaching. | Bible. New Testament—Prophecies—Study and teaching. | End of the world—Study and teaching.
Classification: LCC BT207 .J44 2025 | DDC 232—dc23/eng/20240822
LC record available at https://lccn.loc.gov/2024035364

Scripture quotations are from the (NASB®) New American Standard Bible®. Copyright © 1960, 1971, 1977, 1995 by The Lockman Foundation. Used by permission. All rights reserved. www.lockman.org

Portions of this text have been adapted from *Jesus Revealed in the End Times: Hope for Today from the One Who Holds Our Future* (Grand Rapids: Baker Books, 2025).

Published in association with Yates & Yates, www.yates2.com.

Baker Publishing Group publications use paper produced from sustainable forestry practices and postconsumer waste whenever possible.

25 26 27 28 29 30 31   7 6 5 4 3 2 1

CONTENTS

Introduction and Tips for Study Groups   7

1. Jesus the Subject of Prophecy   11

2. Jesus the Messiah   21

3. Jesus the Prophet   33

4. Jesus the Lamb   43

5. Jesus the Conqueror   53

6. Jesus the King   65

7. Jesus the Judge   77

8. Jesus the Lord   89

9. Jesus Our Friend   99

About Dr. Robert Jeffress   109
About *Pathway to Victory*   111

INTRODUCTION
AND TIPS
FOR STUDY GROUPS

Before beginning your personal or group study of *Jesus Revealed in the End Times: Hope for Today from the One Who Holds Our Future*, please take time to read these introductory comments.

If you are working through the study on your own, you may want to adapt certain sections (for example, the icebreakers) and record your responses to the questions in this study guide or, if preferred, a separate notebook. You might find it more enriching or motivating to study with a partner with whom you can share answers or insights.

If you are leading a group, you may want to ask group members to read one chapter from *Jesus Revealed in the End Times* and work through the corresponding questions in this study guide before each meeting. This isn't always easy for busy adults, so encourage group members with occasional phone calls, emails, or texts between meetings. Help group members manage their time by pointing out that they can cover a few pages each day. Also, encourage them to identify a regular time of the day or week they can devote to the study. They, too, may write their responses to the questions in this study guide or in a separate notebook.

Each session in this study guide includes the following features:

- **Session Topic**—a brief statement summarizing the session.
- **Icebreakers**—activities to help group members get better acquainted with the session topic and/or with one another.
- **Group Discovery Questions**—questions to encourage group participation or individual discovery.
- **Personal Application Questions**—an aid to applying the knowledge gained through study to personal living. (Note: these are important questions for group members to answer for themselves, even if they do not wish to discuss their responses in the meeting.)
- **Optional Activities**—supplemental applications that will enhance the study.
- **Prayer Focus**—suggestions to turn learning into prayer.
- **Assignment**—activities or preparation to complete prior to the next session.

Here are a few tips that can help you more effectively lead small group studies:

1. *Pray for each group member during the week.* Ask the Lord to help you create an open atmosphere where everyone will feel free to share with one another.
2. *Ensure each group member has the* Jesus Revealed in the End Times *book and study guide.* Encourage each group member to bring his or her book and study guide, a pen or pencil, and a Bible to each session. This study is based on the New American Standard Bible (1995), but it is good to have several Bible translations on hand for purposes of comparison.
3. *Start and end on time.* This is especially important for the first meeting because it will set the pattern for the rest of the sessions.
4. *Begin each study session with prayer.* Ask the Holy Spirit to open hearts and minds and to give understanding so that truth will be applied.
5. *Involve everyone in the group discussion.* As learners, we retain some of what we hear and see, but we remember much more of what we hear, see, and do.

6. *Promote a relaxed environment.* If the group is meeting in person, arrange the chairs in a circle or semicircle. This allows eye contact among members and encourages dynamic discussion. Be relaxed in your attitude and manner, and be willing to share with the group.

Jesus the Subject of Prophecy

Session Topic

Jesus was the object of every biblical writer's pen, whether they knew His name or not. It was Jesus the prophets had in mind when they wrote about the Messiah's first coming and the King's second coming. Jesus was the agent for the creation of the world (Col. 1:15–16), and He will be the focus of the end of the world (Rev. 22:20). To put it simply, the world begins and ends with Jesus Christ!

He is the Alpha and Omega, the beginning and the end. He is Lord over our past, our present, and our future. And that glorious vision of Jesus should fill each of us with everlasting hope.

Icebreakers (Choose One)

1. What interested you in joining this study of *Jesus Revealed in the End Times*, and what do you hope to gain as a result of this study?

2. Have you studied biblical prophecy before? What is your attitude toward prophecy?

Group Discovery Questions

1. What comes to your mind when you hear the name Jesus Christ?

2. According to the author, "Jesus of Nazareth is arguably the most widely depicted person in history." Describe some depictions of Jesus you've seen in books, paintings, plays, or movies. How have those depictions influenced your mental image of Jesus? How do you think those depictions have affected the way our culture views Jesus?

3. When you think about Jesus, do you tend to picture Him as He appeared on earth during His first coming, or do you tend to picture the risen Jesus as He currently is, in heaven? Read Revelation 1:12–18 and discuss what you learn about the glorified Christ. How did the apostle John respond when he saw Jesus in His splendor and majesty? How do you think you would have responded?

4. Consider the author's statement: "As important as it is for us to be aware of God's plans for the future, I'm concerned that some believers have become so preoccupied with piecing together the *specifics* of the end times that they've perhaps lost sight of the *subject* of the end times—Jesus Christ Himself." Do you agree or disagree? How would our perspectives and attitudes about the future be affected by focusing less on the *events* of the end times and more on the *Person* who is in charge of those events?

5. Discuss what you learned in this chapter about the difference between the *heady* aspect of biblical prophecy and the *heartfelt* aspect of biblical prophecy. Why are both needed?

6. According to the author, what's the difference between the *last days* and the *end times*? Based on what you learned in this chapter, which one are we in now, and why?

7. Read Colossians 3:1–4 and 2 Peter 3:10–14. How do you think this study of Jesus revealed in the end times could motivate us toward a hopeful attitude and holy living?

Personal Application Questions

1. How often do you think about the end times—constantly, often, sometimes, rarely, or never?

2. What is your attitude toward prophecy? Do you tend to think of biblical prophecy as confusing or irrelevant, or do you tend to make studying prophecy a priority? Explain your answer.

3. Consider the author's statement: "Most people don't live in growing anticipation of the future but in increasing apprehension of what's ahead." When you think about the future, what emotions do you experience? In what ways would you like your perspective on the future to be influenced by this study?

4. The author described both the *heady* aspect and the *heartfelt* aspect of biblical prophecy. Which perspective do you tend to favor more, and why? How can you be more intentional to include both aspects of prophecy as you continue this study?

5. Read Matthew 24:42–44. If Jesus were to return today, would you be ready? Why or why not?

6. Of the eight roles of Jesus Christ mentioned in this chapter's overview of the book (*Messiah*, *Prophet*, *Lamb*, *Conqueror*, *King*, *Judge*, *Lord*, and *Friend*), which one are you most interested in studying, and why?

7. Read Revelation 22:13 and write out Jesus's words in the space below. In what ways can this truth about Jesus influence your perspective on your circumstances?

Optional Activities

1. Break into groups of two or three. Imagine you are having lunch with a Christian friend who is worried about the end times. Take turns role-playing what you would say to encourage your friend to be hopeful about the future, based on what you've learned in today's lesson.

2. Look at a news website or app and read a few headlines of recent world events. In what ways does your perspective of those events change when you consider them in light of what you've learned about Jesus in today's lesson?

Prayer Focus

Thank God for being the One who controls all that is, was, and ever will be. Confess any anxiety you may feel about the future, and ask Him to give you a new sense of calm and courage as you focus on the risen, glorified, and sovereign Jesus Christ during this study.

Assignment

1. This week, remind yourself every day that Jesus is coming soon! For example, you could set a reminder on your smartphone, write in your daily calendar, or place notes around your home and office that say, "Jesus might come today!" Consider how this eternal perspective influences your daily attitudes and activities, and be prepared to share your insights with the group next week.

2. Read chapter 2 of *Jesus Revealed in the End Times* and work through the corresponding study.

Jesus the Messiah

Session Topic

To know Jesus as He really is now and as we'll see Him when He comes again, we first need to understand His role as the Messiah.

In this chapter, we will see that Jesus the Messiah was promised in the Old Testament and heralded when He rode into Jerusalem. Yet within a matter of days, the people's songs of commendation turned into shouts of condemnation.

Because Israel rejected their Messiah, the Lord set aside the nation for a time and began a new work through those who put their faith in Jesus—the church. This chapter addresses significant aspects of these last days and challenges those of us who claim Jesus as Messiah to live a life of godliness this side of the rapture.

Icebreakers (Choose One)

1. Open a kids' jigsaw puzzle (24–36 pieces) and remove about half the pieces from the box. Then distribute the remaining pieces among group members and instruct them to assemble the puzzle together. How do the missing pieces affect your group's perspective of the picture and ability to complete the puzzle? (If time allows, group members can finish the puzzle.) Discuss: How is assembling a puzzle without all the pieces similar to studying the Bible without reading the Old Testament? How could these "missing pieces" of our Bible reading affect our perspective of Jesus and ability to comprehend God's plan?

2. Describe a time when a person, place, or situation was different from what you expected, but your experience ended up better than you thought it would be. Was it easy or challenging for you to adjust your expectations to fit the reality?

Group Discovery Questions

1. According to the author, "The Hebrew word translated as 'Messiah' (*mashiach*) and the Greek word translated as 'Christ' (*Christos*) both mean the same thing: 'Anointed One.'" What did you learn this week about the purpose of anointing in the Bible? Read Exodus 30:30; 1 Samuel 16:1, 12–13; and 1 Kings 19:15–16 and discuss what you learn about these "anointed ones." Who was anointed and for what purpose?

2. The Old Testament prophesied an ultimate Anointed One who would fulfill all God's promises to Israel. Read Isaiah 53 and discuss this description of the anticipated Messiah.

3. In this chapter, the author described five testimonies in the Gospels that clearly identify Jesus as the promised Messiah (*John the Baptist*, *Jesus*, *Peter*, *Martha*, and *the Pharisees*). Which of these declarations of Jesus as the promised Messiah stands out to you most, and why?

4. Discuss the author's statement: "We shouldn't just think of the messiahship of Jesus as a past feature of His life that was fulfilled at the cross. The best is yet to come!" What are some biblical prophecies concerning the Messiah that haven't yet been fulfilled but will be finally and fully achieved by Jesus in the end times? (See, for example, Ps. 2:2, 7–9; Isa. 9:7; 11:1–5; Jer. 23:5; Amos 9:11–15.)

5. God promised not only to give Israel a *Messiah* but also to give Israel a *land* over which the Messiah would rule. Read Genesis 12:1–7 and 13:14–17 and discuss what you learn about the land God promised to Abraham. (See also Gen. 15:18–21; 17:8; 26:1–5; 35:9–15; 50:24.)

6. Read Ezekiel 36:22, 24. How was this prophecy partially fulfilled on May 14, 1948, when the nation of Israel was formally recognized? According to Exodus 23:31 and Joshua 1:4, what are the full geographical boundaries of the land God gave to Israel?

7. Read 1 Kings 8:56 and Romans 11:26–29. Why is it significant that God's promises to Israel are irrevocable? (Look up *irrevocable* in a dictionary if needed.) What does this indicate about God's promises to non-Jewish members of Christ's church?

Personal Application Questions

1. Look up the word *messiah* in a dictionary and write out what you learn.

2. According to the author, "Many Old Testament prophecies relate to [Jesus's] first coming as Israel's Messiah, and all of these were fulfilled to the letter." Read Isaiah 7:14; Hosea 6:2; Micah 5:2; and Zechariah 9:9 and note how Jesus fulfilled these prophecies.

3. Read Matthew 1:1. How does the first verse of the first Gospel introduce Jesus to the world? (See also Matt. 1:18.) Based on what you've learned in this chapter, why is that significant?

4. According to John 1:11, how did the Jewish people respond to Jesus during His first coming? Why do you think they responded to Him in that way?

5. Read Isaiah 61:1–3 and Daniel 7:13–14. What do you learn from these prophecies about Jesus's continued role as Messiah in the end times?

6. Why do you think Titus 2:13 calls the return of Jesus the Messiah our "blessed hope"?

7. Consider the author's statement: "Pondering the imminent return of Jesus the Messiah increases our motivation and optimism each day. It deepens our patience and decreases our irritability. It gives us the blessing of contemplating the future with peace, pleasure, and excitement." Do you agree or disagree? In what ways would your own attitudes and actions be different if you pondered "the imminent return of Jesus the Messiah" every day? Be as specific as possible.

Optional Activities

1. Read Philippians 3:20–21; James 5:7–8; 1 Peter 1:13; 2 Peter 3:11–12; and Jude 21. According to these verses, what should our attitude be considering the return of Jesus the Messiah in the end times? Consider practical ways you can begin to develop that attitude, starting this week.

2. Break into groups of two or three. Read Psalm 122:6–8, and then pray together for the peace of Jerusalem and the nation of Israel. Ask God to give His people, the Jews, not only physical blessing but also eternal blessing by softening their hearts (Rom. 11:25) so they will accept Jesus as their Messiah and know the joy of salvation.

Prayer Focus

Thank God for keeping His promises to Israel and to you. Ask Him to soften the hearts of His people, the Jews, to accept Jesus as their Messiah and be saved. Praise Him for giving you many promises of hope, including the joy you will experience when you and your loved ones "shall always be with the Lord"—Jesus the Messiah—for eternity (1 Thess. 4:17).

Assignment

1. This week, do something tangible to increase your anticipation of the return of Jesus the Messiah. For example, plan your trip to heaven the way you'd plan a vacation. Look up information about the destination. Take screenshots of photos that remind you of heaven. Make a list of things you want to do and people you want to see in heaven. At the end of the week, reflect on how this anticipation of your eternal destination affected your everyday attitudes, motivations, and perspectives.

2. Read chapter 3 of *Jesus Revealed in the End Times* and work through the corresponding study.

3

Jesus the Prophet

Session Topic

During His earthly life, Jesus said many profound and astonishing things. Everything He said was absolute truth, which is why we can trust Him with everything about our future. He knows all the details to come, for He is our all-knowing God whose knowledge of the future is as complete as His knowledge of the past.

Jesus described the future in His Olivet Discourse in Matthew 24–25. Just before His crucifixion, He sat on the Mount of Olives overlooking Jerusalem and the magnificent temple and predicted Israel's future. Some of His prophecies are now history to us, while others will be fulfilled in the end times. Like all the prophecies of the Bible, the ones that have already been fulfilled give us confidence in the reliability of the prophecies that are yet to be fulfilled. This chapter distinguishes past from future events, explains how Israel and the church fit into Jesus's prophecies, and encourages us to prepare for increasingly difficult days before the end times.

Icebreakers (Choose One)

1. What are some predictions about the future you've heard, such as artificial intelligence, global warming, and so on? Are these predictions a cause for celebration, concern, or both?

2. Have you ever made a prediction about something or someone? Did your prediction end up being true or false? Explain what happened.

Group Discovery Questions

1. Read Luke 7:16; John 6:14; and Acts 3:22; 7:37. What do you learn in these verses about Jesus?

2. During His three years of ministry on earth, Jesus correctly predicted many things that took place just as He said. Read Matthew 26:21; 17:22; 20:19; and Mark 9:31. What did Jesus predict in these verses? Review the author's list in *Jesus Revealed in the End Times* ("The Prophet Who Is Always Right") and discuss additional prophecies Jesus made that came true during His earthly ministry. What do these fulfilled prophecies tell you about Jesus the Prophet?

3. During His ministry on earth, Jesus also prophesied things that have not yet taken place. Read John 14:1–3 and describe Jesus's prediction in this passage, which some Bible scholars say refers to the rapture of the church. Read 1 Corinthians 15:51–58 and 1 Thessalonians 4:13–18 and discuss what you learn about this future time when Christians will be "caught up" (Greek *harpazo*, Latin *rapturo*) to be with the Lord.

4. According to Matthew 24:3–13, what are the five signs Jesus said will precede His return? In what ways are we beginning to see these signs take place in these last days?

5. What prophecy did Jesus give about the end times in Matthew 24:14? Discuss specific ways group members can take part in fulfilling this prophecy.

6. Read Matthew 24:27, 29–31 and discuss what you learn from Jesus's prediction of His second coming.

7. According to Matthew 24:42, what should our response be to Jesus's prophecies about the end times?

Personal Application Questions

1. How do you envision the world your children and grandchildren will be facing a half century from now?

2. Read Revelation 1:1. What does this verse reveal to us about Jesus the Prophet? Where did His prophetic message come from, and to whom was this prophetic message given?

3. The author said, "Everything Jesus said came true exactly as He predicted. That fills us with hope and encourages us to be absolutely confident that all His other predictions will come true, including the ones He proclaimed about the events surrounding His return!" Which of Jesus's predictions about the future are you looking forward to being fulfilled?

4. Consider the author's statement: "Paul presented the rapture in 1 Thessalonians 4:13–18 as an imminent event. No passage in the Bible predicts that any other event must take place before the rapture, making it the next episode on God's prophetic calendar. This should give us a sense of excitement every day." Are you excited about and ready for Jesus's imminent return? Why or why not?

5. According to Romans 5:9; 1 Thessalonians 1:10; 5:9; and Revelation 3:10, will Christians experience the wrath of God poured out on the world during the end times? Why or why not?

6. Read Zechariah 9:14 and Matthew 24:27. What did Jesus predict about His second coming in these verses? Why is this significant?

7. Ephesians 5:15–16 says, "Be careful how you walk, not as unwise men but as wise, making the most of your time, because the days are evil." What are some practical things you can do (or stop doing) to "[make] the most of your time" in light of the imminent return of Jesus Christ?

Optional Activities

1. Read Matthew 24:14. Think of a foreign missionary or international missions organization your group could support with prayer, and possibly also a financial gift, as a way to participate in preaching the gospel to all the nations before the end comes.

2. In the daily grind of life, it's easy to grow complacent and view biblical prophecies of the end times as curiosities that don't have anything to do with life in the here and now. Break into groups of two or three and discuss how Jesus's prophecies of the future can affect your life now. Be as specific as possible.

Prayer Focus

Thank God for the wonderful future He has planned for all those who love Him. Confess any worry or dread you may be experiencing about the future. Ask Him to help you to remember the many things Jesus the Prophet revealed about the end times and to eagerly anticipate the day when He will "come again and receive you to Myself, that where I am, there you may be also" (John 14:3).

Assignment

1. In 1 Thessalonians 4:17–18, Paul said about the rapture, "So we shall always be with the Lord. Therefore comfort one another with these words." Think of somebody you know who would be comforted by this promise, and reach out to that person this week to share words of comfort and hope about Jesus's certain and soon return.

2. Read chapter 4 of *Jesus Revealed in the End Times* and work through the corresponding study.

Jesus the Lamb

Session Topic

In Israel's history, lambs were sacrificial animals, serving as stand-ins for Jesus Christ, the perfect Lamb of God whose sacrifice forever paid the debt of sinners who came to the tabernacle and later to the temple for forgiveness. At the beginning of Jesus's earthly ministry, John the Baptist announced, "Behold, the Lamb of God who takes away the sin of the world!" (John 1:29).

Later, another John—the apostle—saw Jesus enthroned as "the Lion that is from the tribe of Judah . . . and . . . a Lamb standing, as if slain" (Rev. 5:5–6). The One who redeemed us now reigns on His throne at the right hand of the Father. Because of His sinless life and perfect obedience, Jesus alone is worthy to take the scroll of God's wrath and break the seals to reveal God's judgment on the unredeemed of the earth during the tribulation. This chapter explores the nature and purpose of these seals, reveals how the Lamb will redeem those who turn to Him in faith during the tribulation, and presents the gospel clearly so we might escape the wrath of the Lamb by having our names written in the Lamb's Book of Life.

No wonder we often borrow the song the angels will sing when the Lamb receives the scroll: "Worthy is the Lamb" (v. 12).

Icebreakers (Choose One)

1. Have you ever interacted with a lamb, perhaps on a farm, a petting zoo, or some other place? Describe your observations of sheep and any experience (or lack thereof) you have with them.

2. Has anyone ever paid for something on your behalf—such as picking up your tab, buying something for you, or covering your expenses for an activity? If so, describe the situation and the effect that person's generosity had on you.

Group Discovery Questions

1. Read Exodus 12:1–13, 21–27 and discuss what you learn about the Passover lamb. Then look up Mark 14:12; Luke 22:7–8; and 1 Corinthians 5:7 and discuss how the Passover lamb is connected to Jesus.

2. In Isaiah 53:7–8, what imagery is used to describe Israel's coming Suffering Servant? Read Acts 8:30–35 and discuss how this imagery is connected to Jesus.

3. According to John 1:29, how did John the Baptist introduce Jesus to the world? (See also v. 36.) Why is this significant?

4. According to Hebrews 10:1–4, what was the purpose of the Old Testament animal sacrifices? Read verses 10–14, 17–18 and discuss what you learn about the sacrifice made by Jesus the Lamb.

5. In Revelation 5, we see the resurrected Jesus revealed in His
   continued role as the Lamb. In verses 1–4, what situation caused
   the apostle John to "weep greatly"? According to verses 5–14, who
   was able to solve this problem, and why? Based on what you've
   learned in this chapter, why do you think it was repeatedly pointed
   out that this Lamb had been "slain" (vv. 6, 9, 12; see also 13:8)?

6. Discuss the author's statement: "Let me pause here to remind you
   why Jesus the Lamb is pouring out His wrath on the world. It's not
   from an evil intent. His desire is twofold: first, to draw and drive
   men and women to Himself for eternal salvation; and second, to
   judge the evil that has devastated the world." Do you think the
   wrath of the Lamb poured out during the end times is a good
   thing or a bad thing? Explain your answer. (See also Gen. 18:25;
   Ps. 7:11; Luke 18:7–8; Rom. 3:5–6; 2 Pet. 3:9.)

7. Read Revelation 19:7–9 and discuss what these verses tell us about
   the marriage of the Lamb. Who is the bride of the Lamb?
   (See Eph. 5:25–27.)

Personal Application Questions

1. According to Exodus 29:38–42 and Leviticus 23:12, 18–19, what are some ways lambs were used as sacrificial animals in the Old Testament law?

2. Read Genesis 22:1–8. In this passage, what was Abraham planning to do? Notice Isaac's question in verse 7 and Abraham's response in verse 8. What possible connections can you see between this story and the future sacrifice of Jesus the Lamb?

3. According to Ezekiel 46:4, 13, what characteristic was required of animals selected to be sacrifices to God? In Hebrews 9:14, how does the writer connect Jesus to this requirement?

4. Read 1 Peter 1:18–19. What does this passage teach about Jesus the Lamb?

5. As you learn about the seven seals, seven trumpets, and seven bowl judgments described in the book of Revelation, why is it important for you to keep your eyes on the Lamb? What perspective does this give you on the various judgments poured out on unbelievers and on evil throughout the book of Revelation?

6. Is your name written in the Lamb's Book of Life? Why or why not?

7. Do you feel like Fiona, the lonely sheep mentioned at the beginning of this chapter? If so, the Lamb of God is searching for you, and He's ready to rescue you, pull you out of your distress, clean you up, care for you, and prepare you for your forever home! Spend a few minutes in prayer, confessing anything that may have been keeping you away from God and telling Him you're ready to come to Him right now.

Optional Activities

1. Read the heavenly anthems of worship of Jesus the Lamb recorded in Revelation 5:11–14. Using what you've learned in this chapter, write your own anthem of worship to Jesus the Lamb.

2. Break into groups of two or three and read the description of the marriage of the Lamb in Revelation 19:7–9. Share with one another what you are looking forward to when Jesus the Lamb is joined to His bride, the church, in a glorious way. Who can you invite to join you in this wedding by sharing with them the gospel of salvation? Pray for these unbelievers, and ask God to give you opportunities to share the gospel so they, too, can be part of this celebration.

Prayer Focus

Thank God for sending Jesus, the Lamb of God who is our ultimate, once-for-all sacrifice for sin. Ask Him to give you opportunities to share the message of salvation with others as you look forward to the day when Jesus the Lamb will finally use His righteous, holy, judicial wrath to rid the world of sinful, diabolical wrong.

Assignment

1. Memorize Revelation 5:12: "Worthy is the Lamb that was slain to receive power and riches and wisdom and might and honor and glory and blessing." To hear these words set to music, you can listen to or watch a YouTube video of "Worthy Is the Lamb That Was Slain" from Handel's *Messiah*.

2. Read chapter 5 of *Jesus Revealed in the End Times* and work through the corresponding study.

Jesus the Conqueror

Session Topic

The Jewish people expected the Messiah to be a conqueror who would overthrow the Roman Empire. They didn't understand that at His first appearing, Jesus came to conquer sin and death—to redeem Israel and all who would believe so we might, in the words of John, "be called children of God" (1 John 3:1). However, at His second coming, Jesus will descend as the Conqueror. He will overthrow His enemies and inaugurate an earthly kingdom that will endure for a thousand years. This chapter explains these events and reminds us that our perception is often deceptive. It may appear that Satan is winning the battle between good and evil, but we can have hope because Christ our Conqueror will deal a death blow to evil at His second coming.

Icebreakers (Choose One)

1. Why do you think our culture enjoys stories in which the good guys win—such as war films, westerns, and action/superhero movies? Name a few examples of popular books, shows, or movies in which a good "conqueror" is victorious over an evil "villain."

2. Have you or has someone in your family served in the military? (If so, thank you for your service!) What do you think it would be like to live in a world with no more war?

Group Discovery Questions

1. Read John 8:44; 2 Corinthians 4:4; and 1 John 5:19. What do these verses teach about Satan and his current influence over the world?

2. Revelation 13 describes a world leader who will come to power during the tribulation (after the church has been raptured) and be a reverse mirror image of Jesus—the son of Satan, appearing good but being evil, claiming worldwide dominion, appearing to die and rise again, and wanting to be worshiped. Read Daniel 7:25; 8:24–25; 2 Thessalonians 2:3–4, 8; and Revelation 13:5–6 and discuss what you learn about the coming Antichrist.

3. The Antichrist will be accompanied by a religious figure known as the False Prophet. According to Revelation 13:11–18 and 16:13, what will the False Prophet do when he arises during the tribulation period?

4. Read Revelation 16:13–16 and discuss what you learn about the campaign of Armageddon, which the author calls "the war that will end all wars." Review the eight phases of Armageddon described in *Jesus Revealed in the End Times* ("The War to End All Wars"), which culminate in the glorious appearance of Jesus the Conqueror.

5. Discuss the author's statement: "I think it's a strong possibility that, after the rapture of the church, the United States will ally itself with the Antichrist's revived Roman Empire and our military will take part in the destruction of Jerusalem, reversing our long-standing friendship and alliance with Israel." Do you agree or disagree? Explain your answer.

6. Read Revelation 19:11–16 and discuss what you learn about the second coming of Jesus the Conqueror. (See also 2 Thess. 2:8.)

7. The author said, "No matter how much Satan's influence appears to be growing in our world, we must stand strong and remind ourselves that Satan is *not* going to win this war. The Bible assures us that Satan, the Antichrist, the False Prophet, and all their minions have already lost the war to end all wars—even before it's fought." Discuss specific ways group members can "stand strong" in this world, knowing that Satan will ultimately be defeated by Jesus the Conqueror.

Personal Application Questions

1. The author said, "Armed conflict continues to this day and won't cease until Jesus the Conqueror returns to earth." Have you or someone you know been affected by war? Describe the situation.

2. According to the author, the prefix *anti* can mean "in place of." In this sense, the Antichrist will try to replace Jesus Christ as a different messiah, worthy of worship (Rev. 13:4). Reflect on the things that are most important to you right now. Is there someone or something that is attempting to replace Christ in your heart? If so, what changes will you make to ensure you worship Christ alone?

3. During the end times, Satan will put together an unholy trinity— with Satan replacing God the Father, the Antichrist replacing Christ, and the False Prophet replacing the Holy Spirit. Why do you think Satan tries to mimic God?

4. What are you doing now to shield yourself against Satan's lies? Write specific actions you can take (or continue) to grow in your knowledge of God and His Word, deepen your community with fellow believers, and resist the devil (James 4:7).

5. The author described military and political leaders who "were deceived into believing that the possibility of world peace rests completely in the hands of mere humans. It doesn't. It never has. Such a perception is deceptive and dangerous because it removes God from the equation." Do you agree or disagree? Explain your answer.

6. Consider the author's statement: "Jesus the Conqueror's great victory at His second coming will occur in an instant, while He is descending from heaven, before He reaches earth. It takes longer to describe than it will actually take to fight the battle!" What perspective does this give you on a situation you are struggling with today?

7. In what ways can the Bible's promise of Jesus the Conqueror's ultimate victory over evil help you through even the worst of times right now? Be as specific as possible.

Optional Activities

1. Read Psalm 91 and reflect on this statement from the author: "As you and I face a future that seems to be growing ever darker, we can hold on to this promise of hope and rescue from our sovereign Conqueror!"

2. Break into groups of two or three and discuss ways you see Satan's influence in the world today. What are some practical ways we can stand strong during these evil days and remind ourselves that Satan is *not* going to win this war?

Prayer Focus

Thank God that no matter how much Satan's influence appears to be growing in our world, we know Jesus the Conqueror will win! Ask Him to help you resist Satan's influence and lies, and praise Him that "greater is He who is in you than he who is in the world" (1 John 4:4).

Assignment

1. This week, pay attention to the news and conversations around you, and make a list of some of the ways Satan is influencing our world. Pray about each item on the list, then cross through it and write, "Jesus the Conqueror will win the victory!"

2. Read chapter 6 of *Jesus Revealed in the End Times* and work through the corresponding study.

Jesus the King

Session Topic

Following Jesus's great victory at Armageddon, when He conquers the forces of evil, Jesus will reign in Jerusalem as Israel's promised King for a thousand years. Though it will be a time of universal peace, not everyone who lives in the kingdom will pledge allegiance to King Jesus, leading to a final rebellion and judgment. This chapter answers many of the questions people have about the millennial kingdom and provides a warning that the time of salvation is at hand because a time is coming when it will be too late. Therefore, we who believe must be busy telling others about the salvation offered by the King. This chapter emphasizes a wonderful truth: the kingship of Jesus isn't just a future event. He is your King and mine right now.

Icebreakers (Choose One)

1. Did you watch the coronation of King Charles III? Why do you think so many people are fascinated by the British royals?

2. If you were appointed "king for a day," what would you do?

Group Discovery Questions

1. According to the author, "Many people assume Christ will establish His millennial kingdom immediately after He returns. But the Bible indicates there will be an interim period of two and a half months between the end of the tribulation and the beginning of Jesus's millennial kingdom." Read Daniel 12:11–12. What did you learn from this chapter about events that may take place during the "thirty days" and "forty-five days" between the end of the campaign of Armageddon and the beginning of the millennium?

2. Read Revelation 20:1–6 and discuss what you learn about the millennial kingdom. According to this passage, where will Satan be during the one thousand years of Jesus's reign on earth?

3. According to Revelation 19:20, where will the Antichrist and False Prophet be during the millennial kingdom?

4. The author described two additional resurrections that will take place during this transitional time—the resurrection of Old Testament saints (Isa. 26:19; Dan. 12:2) and the resurrection of tribulation martyrs (Rev. 20:4). Including these two groups, who will enter the millennial kingdom?

5. The author pointed out, "Two groups of saved people will enter the millennial kingdom: those with immortal bodies and those with mortal bodies." Read 1 Corinthians 15:42–44, 50–57 and discuss what you learn about the glorified bodies Christians will receive at the rapture and then other resurrected believers will receive before the millennium. Which group of believers will enter the millennium in their earthly bodies, and why?

6. According to the author, "The millennial kingdom will be like no other epoch in human history. Not only will there be extraordinary spiritual and material blessings, but the geography of the earth will be altered, and God's promises to His covenant people will finally and fully be fulfilled." Discuss what you learned in this chapter about characteristics of the millennial kingdom.

7. According to Revelation 20:7–10, what happens to Satan and his minions at the end of the millennium? Why is this significant?

Personal Application Questions

1. Read Romans 8:18. Whenever you feel weak or sick, how could it help you to remember the glorified body you will enjoy forever?

2. The author said, "To me, the greatest fact regarding the millennial kingdom is that Jesus always keeps His promises." In Matthew 5:18, what did Jesus say about keeping His promises?

3. Read Isaiah 9:7 and 11:3–5. What do you learn from these verses about Jesus the King's government on earth?

4. In Revelation 20:10, the false trinity of Satan, the Antichrist, and the False Prophet are permanently consigned to hell, where they'll be "tormented day and night forever and ever." How can knowing what the devil's future looks like help you the next time the devil troubles you?

5. According to Romans 8:17, if you have proclaimed Jesus as the King of your life, what is your position in relation to Jesus in the coming millennial kingdom?

6. The author said, "The Lord hasn't yet appeared in the sky for the rapture, but it could happen any day now. If He seems to be delaying, it's because He is giving people an opportunity to place their faith in Him." Read 1 Timothy 2:3–4 and 2 Peter 3:9. What do you learn from these verses about God?

7. Are you ready for the last days? Reflect on the author's statement: "Today is the day of salvation. Don't put off this decision because you might not have a tomorrow. Come to Jesus, just as you are. Confess your sins and trust His salvation. When you decide to follow Jesus Christ, it makes all the difference in your life today— and tomorrow."

Optional Activities

1. Listen to the "Hallelujah" chorus from Handel's *Messiah* and focus on the lyrics, which are taken from Revelation 11:15 and 19:6, 16.

2. Break into groups of two or three and share what you are most excited about experiencing in the millennial kingdom.

Prayer Focus

Thank God for sending Jesus to be a King who died for you, rose again, and has a reign that will never end. Ask Him to help you remember that He's on the throne now, no matter what circumstances you may be facing. And praise Jesus the King for His promise that He will come again to sit on an earthly throne for a thousand years and then reign in heaven forever during the new heaven and earth!

Assignment

1. This week, make "Maranatha!" ("Come, Lord Jesus!") a daily prayer as you look forward to Christ's return and your full inheritance in heaven.

2. Read chapter 7 of *Jesus Revealed in the End Times* and work through the corresponding study.

Jesus the Judge

Session Topic

Paul charged Timothy to preach the gospel—to "be ready in season and out of season" (2 Tim. 4:2)—because a time is coming when preaching will cease. That day is the day of judgment when Jesus will "judge the living and the dead" (v. 1). None of us will escape His judgment. The writer of Hebrews put it this way: "It is appointed for men to die once and after this comes judgment" (9:27). However, judgment doesn't come all at the same time, and believers will face a different judgment than unbelievers. This chapter unpacks these judgments—when they will occur, what will happen at the time, and the rewards and punishments that will be distributed. The chapter also encourages us to follow Christ fully in this life, for the rewards in the next life are great indeed!

Icebreakers (Choose One)

1. Name a few courtroom television shows—programs in which court cases are televised and ruled on by a judge, such as *Judge Judy*. Who are some famous television judges? Why do you think these shows are so popular?

2. If you had the chance, would you like to be a US Supreme Court justice? Why or why not?

Group Discovery Questions

1. Do most people today think judgment is a good thing or a bad thing? Explain your answer.

2. Discuss the author's statement: "We must be careful not to think of our Lord's judgment only in negative terms. Yes, He will punish evil, but He will also make sure His faithful people are eternally secure in the joy of their Lord." In what ways could this perspective about judgment (being evaluated to receive rewards, not punishment) change your attitude about facing Jesus the Judge in the future?

3. According to 2 Corinthians 5:10, what is the purpose of the judgment seat of Christ for believers?

4. The author said, "One day soon, Jesus Himself will be sitting on the judgment seat, and His rulings will be both judicial and ceremonial." What is the difference between judicial and ceremonial judgments? In what way is Jesus's future judgment of believers judicial? (See Rom. 14:10.) In what way is the judgment seat of Christ ceremonial? (See 1 Cor. 3:14.)

   Note from the author: "It's important to remember that in this judgment of Christians, the verdict doesn't involve our redemption; our sins have already been judged by God, and His divine punishment was satisfied by Christ on the cross. Rather, Jesus's bema *verdict at the judgment seat of Christ will involve our rewards."*

5. Read 1 Corinthians 3:11–15. What do you learn in this passage about the judgment seat of Christ? Discuss examples of a Christian's actions that might be judged as "gold, silver, precious stones" and works that might be rendered as "wood, hay, straw." What is used to "test the quality of each man's work"?

6. In addition to the judgment seat of Christ (which occurs during the tribulation), this chapter mentions the judgments that will take place at the end of the tribulation for four other groups: tribulation martyrs, Israel, Gentiles, and all unbelievers at the great white throne. What did you learn in your study this week about these judgments?

7. Discuss this statement by the author concerning the great white throne judgment: "When Jesus the Judge fails to find these unbelievers' names recorded in the Book of Life, He will turn to the book of death. When their names are found there, He will pass sentence based upon their earthly deeds, which will be found wanting, and He will rightly condemn them to the lake of fire. As David wrote in Psalm 14:3, 'There is no one who does good, not even one.' [See also Rom. 3:12.] But even if they put up a defense that some of their deeds were good, the Judge will condemn them for falling short of God's holy standard, which renders 'all our righteous deeds [as] a filthy garment' (Isa. 64:6). So there these unbelievers will stand, condemned by their own disbelief and misdeeds, rightly judged by the righteous Judge." What perspective does this give you toward those who think they can do enough good works to earn eternity in heaven?

Personal Application Questions

1. Have you ever been judged on something (athletic event, academic competition, etc.) and won a prize? Did the prize affect your mindset as you performed? Why or why not?

2. At the judgment seat of Christ, Jesus will judge our actions, words, and thoughts. Reflect on some of your own recent actions, words, and thoughts—do you think Jesus would render them good or worthless? Explain your answer.

3. Read Acts 17:30–31. According to the apostle Paul, what is God's message to people today, and why? What can you do to help communicate that message to unbelievers?

4. Bible students through the ages have identified five specific heavenly rewards, or "crowns," in God's Word. Read 1 Corinthians 9:25; 1 Thessalonians 2:19; 2 Timothy 4:8; James 1:12; and 1 Peter 5:1–4 and discuss the crowns described in these verses. Which crown do you hope to receive from Jesus the Judge?

5. Read Matthew 25:31–40. Although our Lord's words in this passage specifically pertain to the tribulation, the principle of extending Christ's love by helping others is something Christians can and should begin practicing now. What are you currently doing (or can you begin doing) to show compassion toward, care for, and meet the needs of those around you? Think of a specific person to whom you can show compassion and care this week.

6. In Jesus's parable of the talents, what did the master say to the faithful slave in Matthew 25:21? Write out this statement below in anticipation of the day when you will stand before Jesus the Judge and desire to hear these words pronounced over you.

7. Are the choices you're making today consistent with what you want to hear when you stand before Jesus the Judge? Why or why not? What changes would you like to make before you appear at the judgment seat of Christ?

Optional Activities

1. Consider the author's statement: "Just as Olympians commit themselves to their sport and discipline themselves in the hope of one day standing on the victor's podium and receiving a medal, faithful followers of Jesus commit themselves to Him and discipline themselves to pursue Him with their whole heart, soul, mind, and strength in the hope of one day receiving a reward from Him (Rev. 22:12)." What are some specific actions you can take to discipline yourself to pursue God fully and faithfully?

2. Break into groups of two or three. Using the biblical truths you've learned in this chapter, role-play how you would respond to someone who says, "I think I'm a good enough person to get into heaven."

Prayer Focus

Thank God for covering you by the blood of Jesus the Lamb so you don't have to tremble in fear of Jesus the Judge. Ask Him to help you remember His justice as it motivates you to live righteously, striving to maintain a disciplined life, seeking to evangelize and disciple others, eagerly awaiting His return, enduring trials and suffering, and tending to the needs of His people.

Assignment

1. Look at your calendar and review your daily activities this week. Is there anything you would like to change or adjust in light of what you've learned about the judgment seat of Christ?

2. Read chapter 8 of *Jesus Revealed in the End Times* and work through the corresponding study.

Jesus the Lord

Session Topic

When the last echo of Christ's gavel rings and everyone has received their rewards or punishment, Jesus will institute a kingdom that will last for eternity, where death and dying, tears and crying will be no more. The New Jerusalem—the heavenly city—will descend on the renewed earth, and all the redeemed of the Lord will enter eternity with glorified bodies to be with the Lord forever. This chapter describes these events and offers us a word of hope that not only is Jesus in full control of our todays, including the events that cause us frustration and fear, but He is also in full control of our eternal future.

Just as all the chapters of the Bible lead to Revelation 21 and 22—the description of the New Jerusalem—so all the days and years of God's children are leading to our heavenly home. In this chapter, we'll be encouraged by the picture we have of eternity.

Icebreakers (Choose One)

1. What are some common misconceptions about what heaven will be like?

2. In what ways has heaven been portrayed in movies, television shows, books, songs, and so forth? Why do you think our culture is fascinated by the afterlife?

Group Discovery Questions

1. What comes to your mind when you think about heaven?

2. Read Revelation 21:1–5. How does this passage describe the new heaven and earth?

3. According to the author, "You'll feel at home in heaven. The new earth will have a familiarity that will set you at ease, for it will be like our old earth, only new, better, fresh, and sinless." How does this realization—that we aren't going to spend eternity in a vapory place somewhere up in the clouds but instead on a completely restored, renewed earth—affect your anticipation of heaven?

4. Read Revelation 21:22–27 and 22:1–5. What do you learn from these passages about the New Jerusalem?

5. According to Revelation 21:3, what will our relationship with God
   be like in the new heaven and earth?

6. Discuss the author's statement: "Everything about the New
   Jerusalem—from the golden streets to the pearly gates to the
   golden walls—will declare the splendor of the Lord. Remember, in
   the end, it's all about Him!" In what ways does your perspective of
   heaven shift when you focus more on "the splendor of the Lord"
   than on the blessings you will experience there?

7. How does what you've learned about the hope of heaven affect
   your perspective of life here and now?

Personal Application Questions

1. Revelation 21:5 says, "Behold, I am making all things new."
   What is something you are struggling with currently that you look
   forward to being made new in eternity?

2. Read Psalm 102:25–26; Isaiah 51:6; 65:17; and 2 Peter 3:7–13.
   What do you learn from these passages about the new heaven
   and earth?

3. The author said, "If this world contains such eye-popping wonders
   now, we can only imagine how beautiful the new heaven and earth
   must be!" Read Psalm 27:4. What do you think it will be like to
   "behold the beauty of the LORD" in heaven for eternity?

4. According to the author, "When we finally get to the eternal state, we'll . . . also experience a new quality to our relationships. With our friends, with the angels, and with the Lord Himself, we'll enjoy the sweetness, intimacy, and satisfaction that are often missing on the old earth." Who are some of the people you are looking forward to seeing in heaven?

5. Read Psalm 36:8 and Revelation 22:1. What are you doing in your life right now to be regularly refreshed and replenished by the Lord?

6. The author said, "I encourage you to trust the Creator of this staggering heavenly city to do tremendous things for you now, for He alone is Lord! One day, you'll see the eternal city in all its glory—but right now, you have 'Christ in you, the hope of glory' (Col. 1:27)." In what area of your life do you need tremendous strength from Jesus the Lord?

7. In what ways are you actively engaged in sharing the gospel with others so they, too, can experience eternity in heaven?

Optional Activities

1. Did you know the popular Christmas carol "Joy to the World" isn't about the birth of Jesus but His second coming and heavenly rule? Look up the lyrics to "Joy to the World," and consider how the words of this familiar song reflect what you've been learning about Jesus revealed in the end times.

2. Break into groups of two or three and discuss what you are most looking forward to experiencing in the new heaven and earth.

Prayer Focus

Thank God that this old earth will pass away and the new heaven and earth will come. Ask Him to help you set your mind on heaven, a place where sin and sickness, decay and death are no more. Praise Him for His promise that you will live forever in the New Jerusalem and experience a new relationship with Him—one where you can speak with Him face-to-face, without guilt and shame. Maranatha! Come, Lord Jesus!

Assignment

1. Make a list of unbelievers you know in your family, workplace, school, and community. Ask God to give you opportunities to talk with them, and commit to sharing the gospel of salvation with them before it's too late.

2. Read chapter 9 of *Jesus Revealed in the End Times* and work through the corresponding study.

Jesus Our Friend

Session Topic

Some Christians are hesitant to relate to Jesus as Friend, thinking that friendship with Jesus somehow diminishes His authority in our lives. Perhaps after reading about how Jesus will be revealed and exalted and glorified in the end times, you think it would be presumptuous to call Him "Friend." After all, how could the triumphant, majestic King of the universe also be your Friend?

As we will see, the closing chapter of the Bible gives us this beautiful insight into the intimacy we will have with Jesus our Friend in our eternal future: "There will no longer be any curse; and the throne of God and of the Lamb will be in it, and His bond-servants will serve Him; they will see His face, and His name will be on their foreheads" (Rev. 22:3–4).

Icebreakers (Choose One)

1. Who was your childhood best friend? Describe that person and share a memory, if you feel comfortable doing so.

2. Think of someone who is a good friend to you or others. What are some of the attitudes and actions that make this person such a good friend?

Group Discovery Questions

1. Do you think today's technology tends to make people more lonely or less lonely? Explain your answer.

2. Read Proverbs 18:24 and John 15:13, 15. What do you learn about Jesus our Friend in these verses?

3. Discuss the author's statement: "Throughout the endless ages of eternity, Jesus isn't going to be a distant and inaccessible monarch. He's not going to sit on a faraway throne behind imposing walls or impenetrable gates. He won't hide His royal presence from us or limit His fellowship with us. Instead, He will also forever be our Friend." Do you find it easy or difficult to imagine Jesus as your Friend? Explain your answer.

4. Read the following verses and notice how often Jesus used the word *friend*: Luke 5:20; 12:4; and John 11:11; 15:13–14. What do Jesus's words of affection for His disciples indicate about His friendship with those of us who follow in their footsteps?

5. How does Revelation 22:3–4 describe the intimacy we will have with Jesus our Friend in eternity?

6. In what ways has your attitude toward biblical prophecy and the end times changed since you began this study?

7. According to the author, "There's something much more important than just knowing *what* is going to happen. It's knowing *Who* is going to come to make it all happen." Review the summary of Jesus's roles in the end times below and discuss which one(s) have stood out to you the most during your study of *Jesus Revealed in the End Times*:

> As the Messiah, Jesus offered Himself as Israel's long-awaited Anointed One. They rejected Him, but He will redeem and provide a kingdom for them.
>
> As the Prophet, Jesus predicted what the future holds for Jews and Gentiles, for those who will enter the millennial kingdom and those who will not.
>
> As the Lamb, Jesus sacrificed Himself to take away sin from the unrighteous. He now sits on His heavenly throne, poised to pour out His wrath on a wicked world.
>
> As the Conqueror, Jesus will return to earth and destroy evil with the word of His mouth.
>
> As the King, Jesus will rule and reign over the earth for a thousand years, bringing with Him peace and healing.
>
> As the Judge, Jesus will evaluate the righteous and the unrighteous, dispensing justice by rewarding the upright and punishing the unholy.
>
> As the Lord, Jesus will redeem what is old and make all things new. He will build a New Jerusalem where all the redeemed, Jews and Gentiles alike, will live for eternity.
>
> And as our Friend, Jesus will be our intimate companion forever and ever.
>
> In the end, it's all about Him!

Personal Application Questions

1. If you're on social media, do your social media friends provide real companionship? Why or why not?

2. Imagine what it would be like to have a friend who knows all about you, always answers when you call, and sticks with you no matter what. In what ways would a friendship like that enhance your life?

3. Are you hesitant to relate to Jesus as Friend, thinking that friendship with Jesus somehow diminishes His authority in your life? If so, consider how Jesus's desire to be your Friend actually magnifies His majesty and glory rather than diminishing it. Why is it significant that Jesus the Lord was also known as "a friend of tax collectors and sinners" (Matt. 11:19)?

4. Read Luke 24:13–27. What stands out to you about this encounter between the risen Jesus and these two followers? What can we learn from this passage about the time when we, too, will be able to walk and talk with our risen Savior?

5. Read 1 Corinthians 13:12 and Philippians 3:10. What desire did Paul express in these verses? Do you also desire to know Christ more deeply and more intimately as your Friend?

6. Consider the author's statement: "If you're suffering from loneliness or a poor self-image and think nobody would be interested in you, remember this: the Creator of the universe is so interested in you—He loves you so much, He desires a relationship with you so much—that He died for you. That's the whole reason for the incarnation. Jesus came to earth and died for you because He values you. He wants a relationship with you. He wants to be your Friend." Ask God to help you believe this truth, and thank Jesus for being your Friend.

7. The author said, "Here's the simple truth: you are not prepared to meet Christ in the future end times until you have met Christ in these present last days." Are you ready?

Optional Activities

1. Are you prepared to meet Christ in the future end times? Review the author's summary of what the Bible tells us about how we can be saved, and then live out that salvation day by day:

   - Accept Jesus as Messiah, the Anointed One.
   - Believe Jesus's prophecies about your eternal future—that heaven awaits those who receive Him, and hell awaits those who reject Him.
   - Trust Jesus as the Lamb of God who takes away your sin.
   - Celebrate Jesus as the Conqueror who destroyed sin and death and will one day return to destroy evil.
   - Honor Jesus as King of your life.
   - Revere Jesus as the Judge who rewards the righteous and punishes the wicked.
   - Worship Jesus as the Lord who makes all things new and provides an eternal home for your forever future.
   - And begin today to live with the continual awareness that Jesus is your Friend.

2. If you would like to become a Christian and know for sure that one day you will be welcomed into heaven, I invite you to pray this prayer, knowing that God is listening:

   Dear God,

   Thank You for loving me. I realize I have failed You in so many ways. And I am truly sorry for the sin in my life. I believe You love me so much that You sent Your Son, Jesus, to die on the cross for me, to take the punishment I deserve for my sin. And right now, I am trusting in what Jesus did for me—not in my good works—to save me from my sins. Thank You for forgiving me. Help me to spend the rest of my life serving You. In Jesus's name, amen.

Prayer Focus

Thank God for the many insights and challenges He has brought to you through this study. Ask Him to help you continue to grow in your understanding of how Jesus is revealed in the end times and to experience a deeper sense of awe for what He has done on your behalf today, as well as what He will do for you tomorrow.

ABOUT DR. ROBERT JEFFRESS

DR. ROBERT JEFFRESS is senior pastor of the sixteen-thousand-member First Baptist Church in Dallas, Texas, and a Fox News contributor. He has made more than four thousand guest appearances on radio and television programs and regularly appears on major mainstream media outlets such as Fox News Channel's *Fox & Friends*, *Hannity*, *Fox News @ Night*, and *Varney & Co.*, as well as HBO's *Real Time with Bill Maher*.

Established in 1996, *Pathway to Victory* exists to pierce the darkness with the light of God's Word through the most effective media available. The daily radio program airs on more than one thousand stations. The daily television program can be seen Monday through Friday and every Sunday on more than eleven thousand cable and satellite systems, including the Trinity Broadcasting Network, where it has been the #1 viewed program since 2020. *Pathway to Victory* broadcasts reach all major markets in the United States plus 195 countries throughout the world. Additionally, *Pathway to Victory* ministers globally through podcasting, social media, and other digital media. On each daily broadcast, Dr. Jeffress provides practical application of God's Word to everyday life through clear, uncompromised biblical teaching.

Dr. Jeffress is the author of more than thirty books, including *Perfect Ending*, *Not All Roads Lead to Heaven*, *A Place Called Heaven*, *Choosing the Extraordinary Life*, *Courageous*, *Invincible*, *18 Minutes with Jesus*, *What Every Christian Should Know*, *Are We Living in the End Times?*, and *The 10*.

Dr. Jeffress graduated with a DMin from Southwestern Baptist Theological Seminary, a ThM from Dallas Theological Seminary, and a BS from Baylor University. In May 2010, he was awarded a Doctor of Divinity degree from Dallas Baptist University. In June 2011, Dr. Jeffress received the Distinguished Alumnus of the Year award from Southwestern Baptist Theological Seminary. He is also an adjunct professor at Dallas Theological Seminary.

Dr. Jeffress and his wife, Amy, have two daughters and three grandchildren.

Connect with Dr. Robert Jeffress:

@DrJeffress

@RobertJeffress

@RobertJeffress

ABOUT *PATHWAY TO VICTORY*

Established in 1996, *Pathway to Victory* serves as the broadcast ministry of Dr. Robert Jeffress. *Pathway to Victory* stands for truth and exists to pierce the darkness with the light of God's Word through the most effective media available, including television, radio, print, and digital media.

Through *Pathway to Victory*, Dr. Jeffress spreads the good news of Jesus Christ to lost and hurting people, confronts an ungodly culture with God's truth, and equips the saints to apply Scripture to their everyday lives. More than a thousand radio stations in the United States broadcast the daily radio program, while Daystar, Trinity Broadcasting Network, and other Christian television networks air *Pathway to Victory* both in the United States and internationally.

Our mission is to provide practical application of God's Word to everyday life through clear, biblical teaching. Our goal is to lead people to become obedient and reproducing disciples of Jesus Christ, as He commanded in Matthew 28:18–20. As our ministry continues to expand, we are confident the Lord will use *Pathway to Victory* to transform the world with God's Word . . . one life at a time.